ULTIMATE RETRO DISCO DANCE PARTY

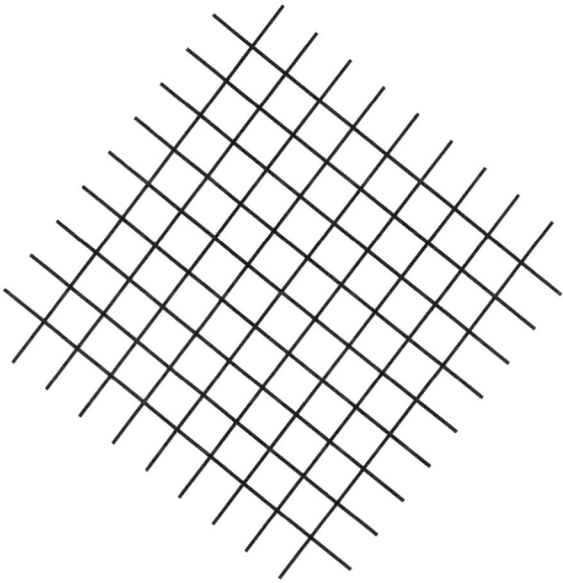

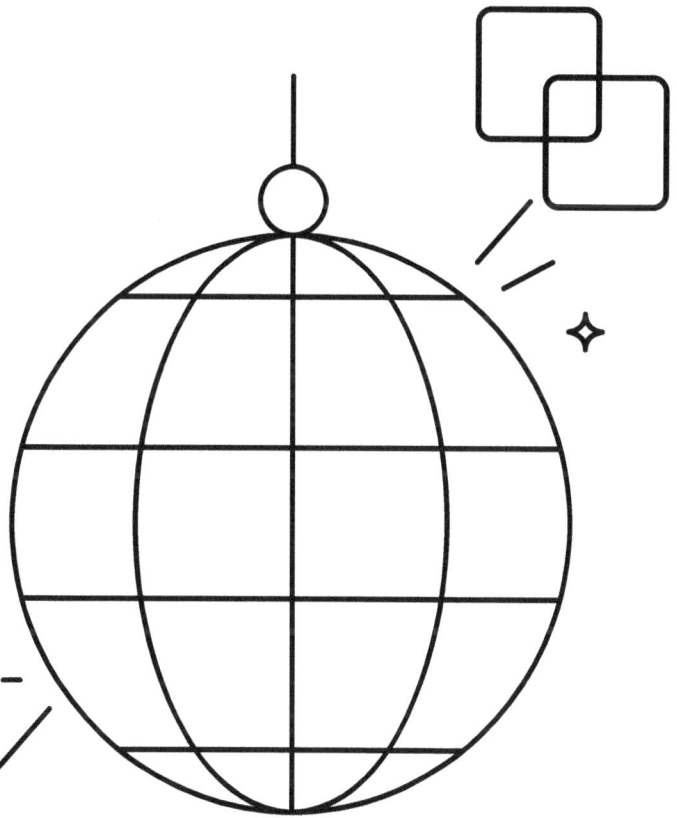

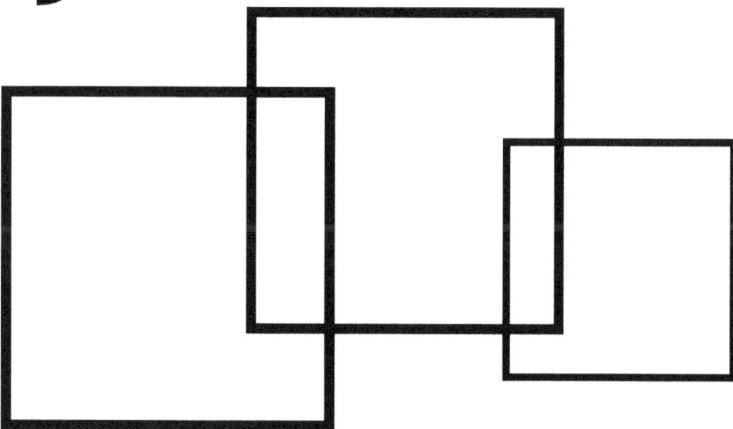

ULTIMATE

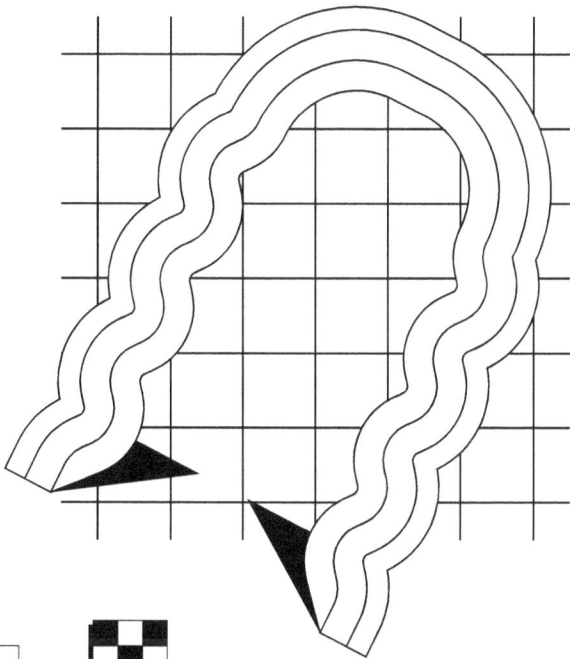

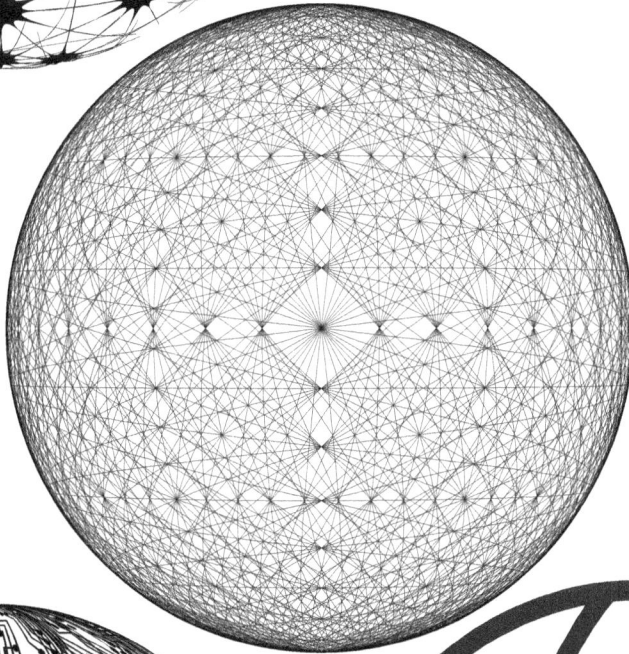

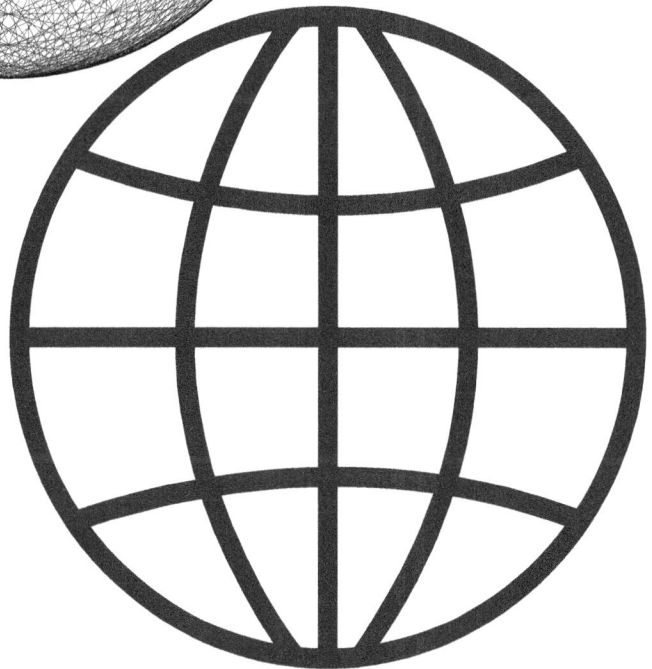

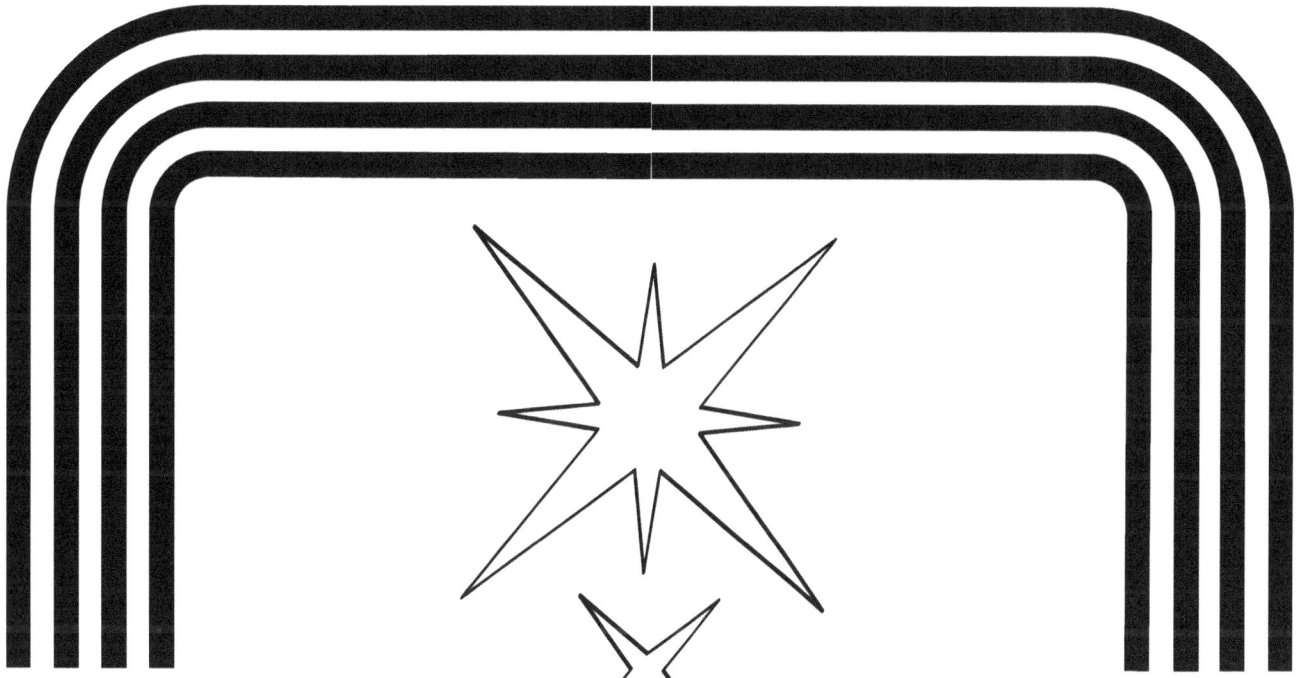

RETRO

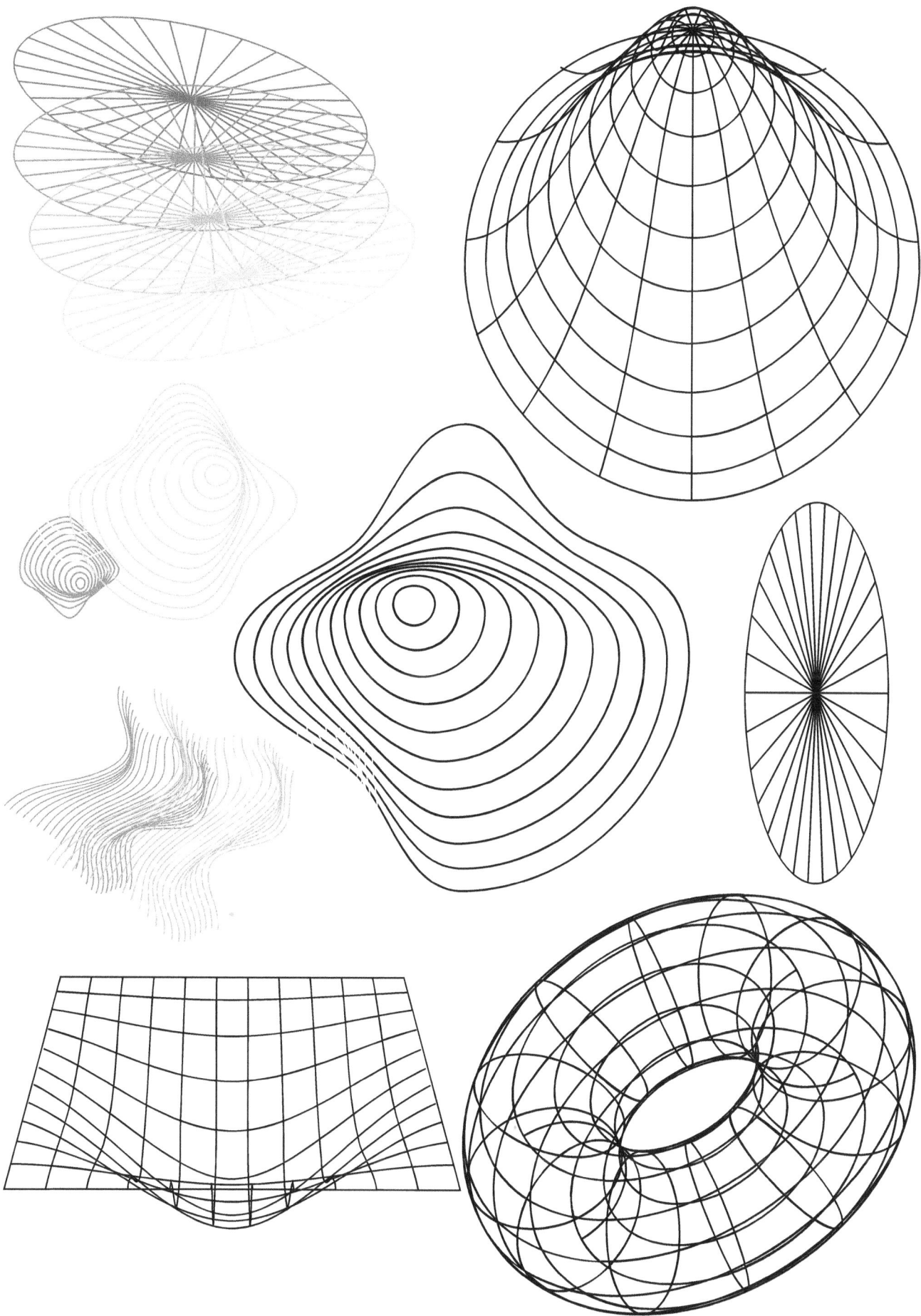

DISCO

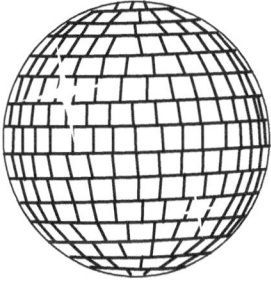 DISCO

DISCO

 DISCO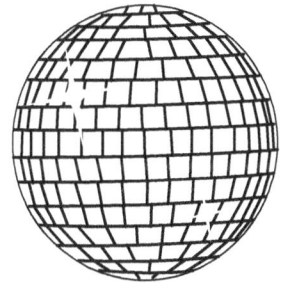

DISCO

 DISCO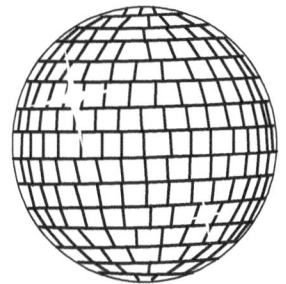

DISCO

good vibes

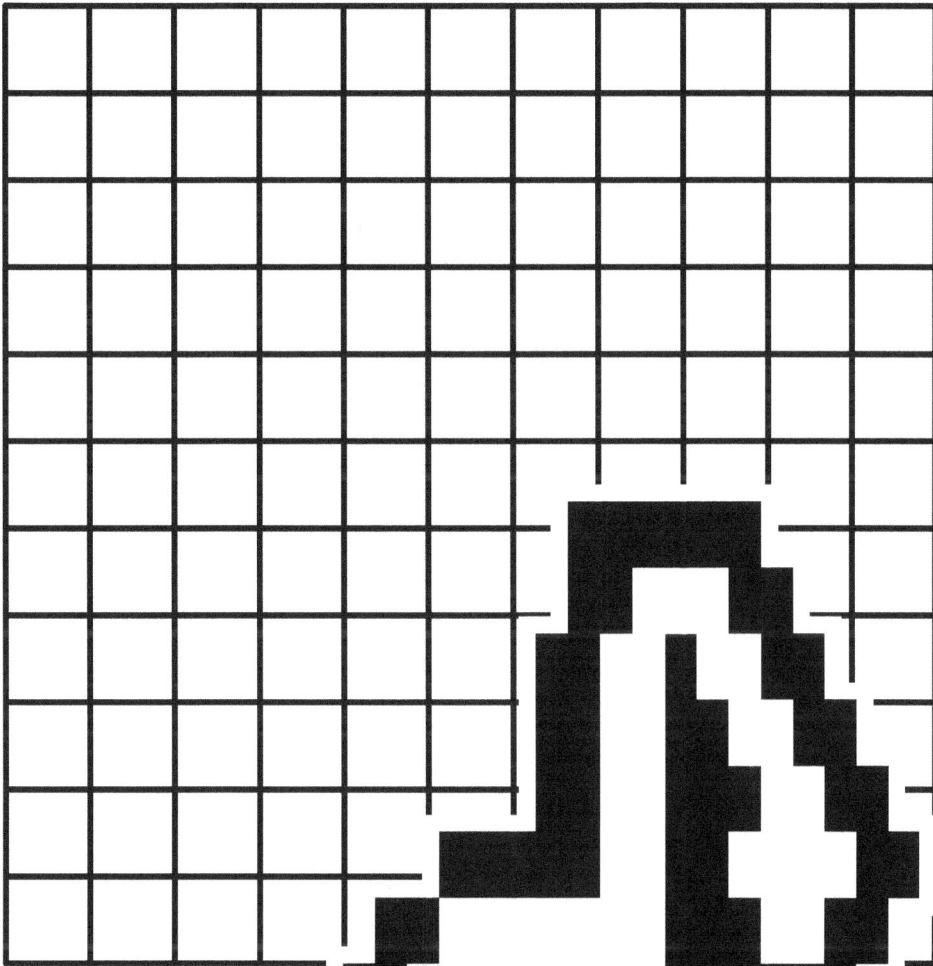

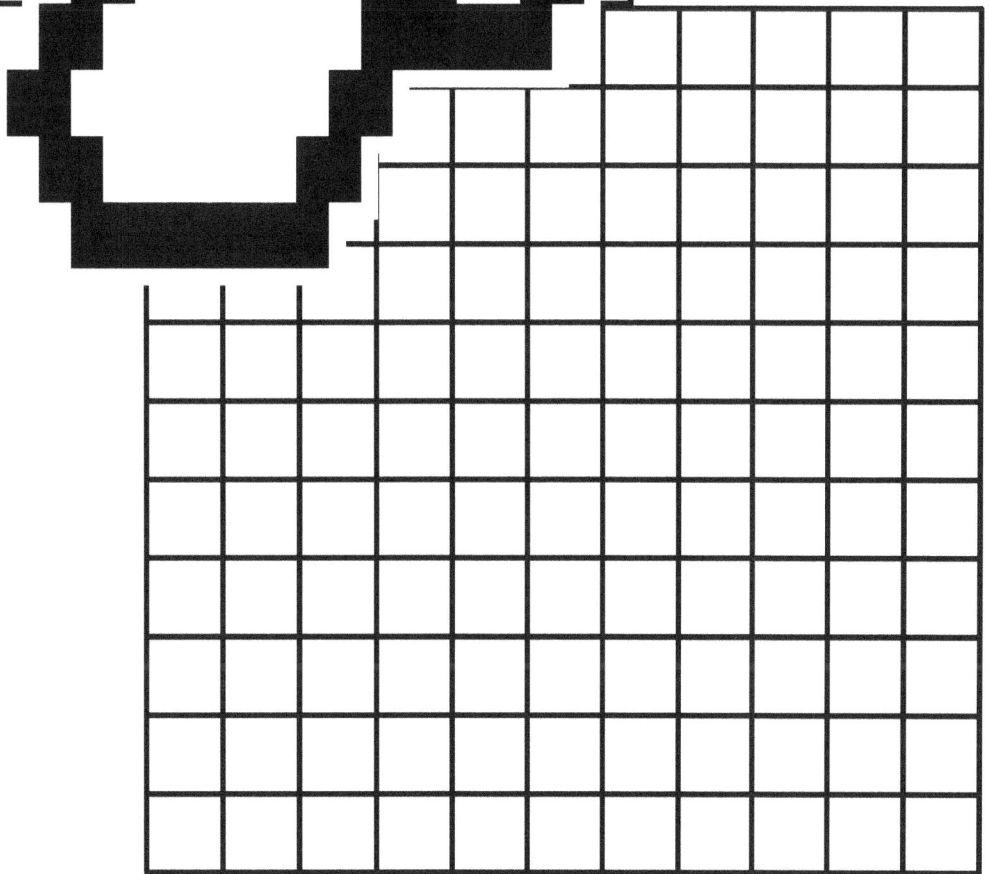

LATE
NIGHT
RETRO

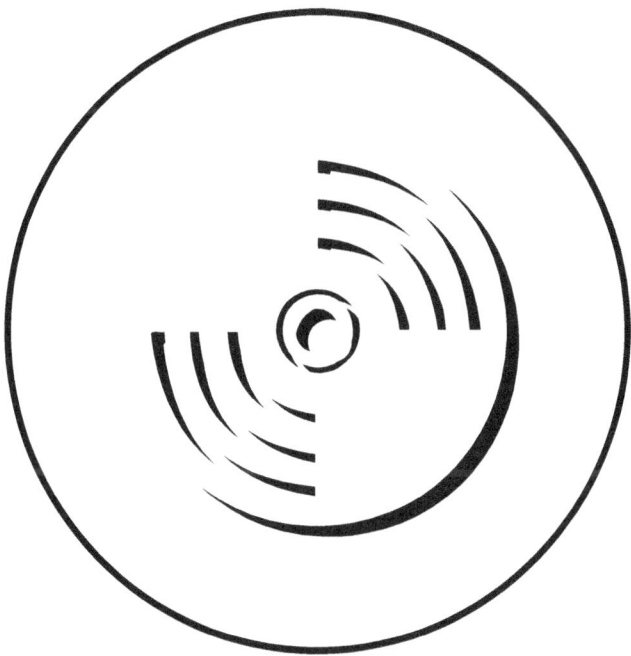

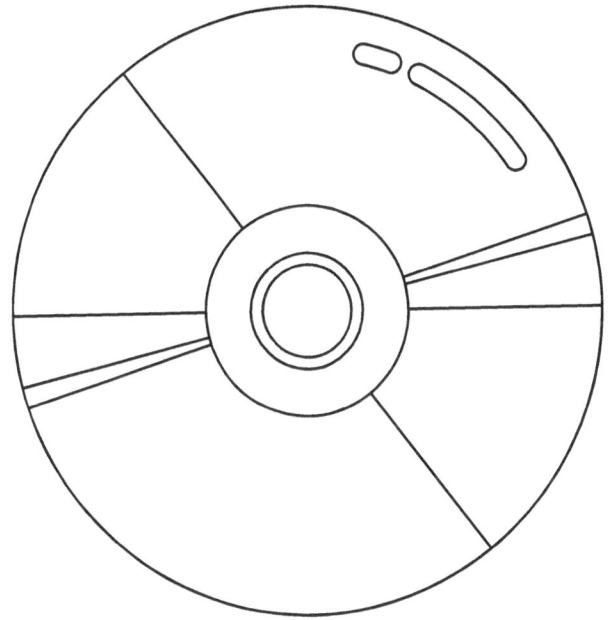

PARTY

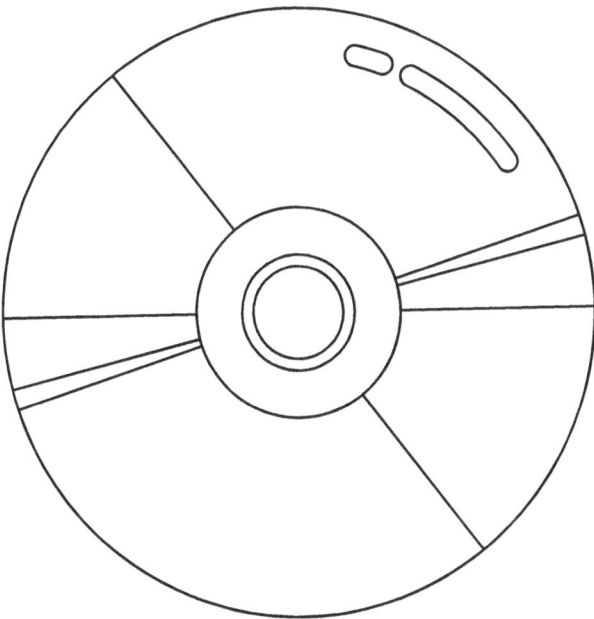

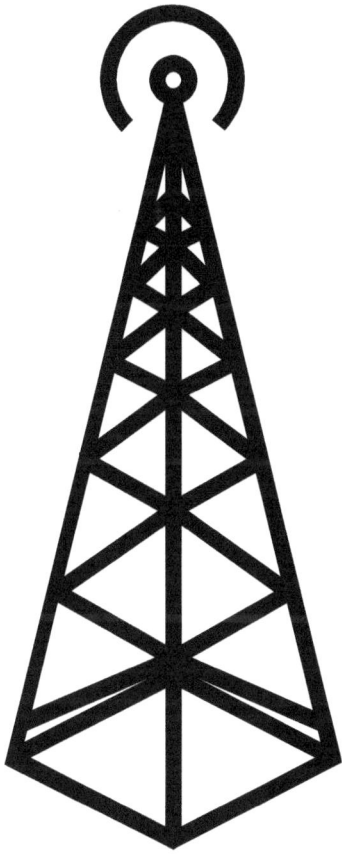

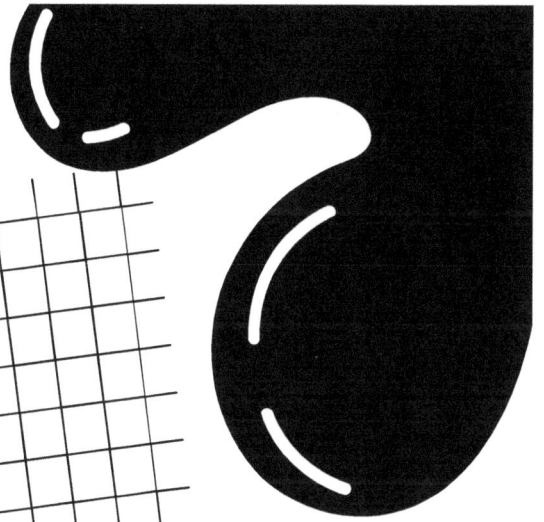

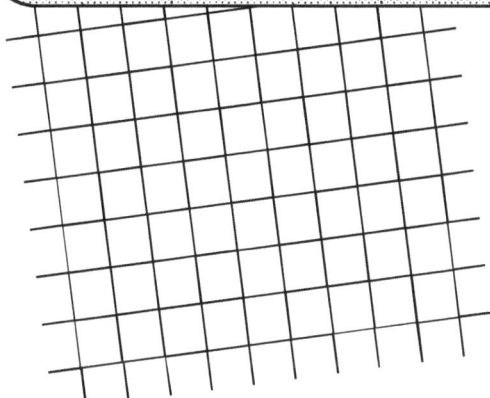

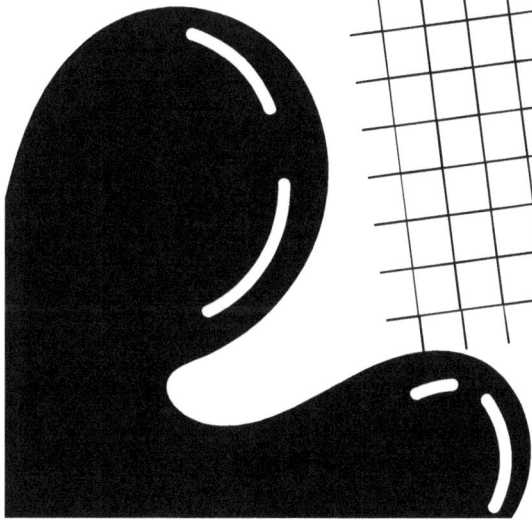

VIBES

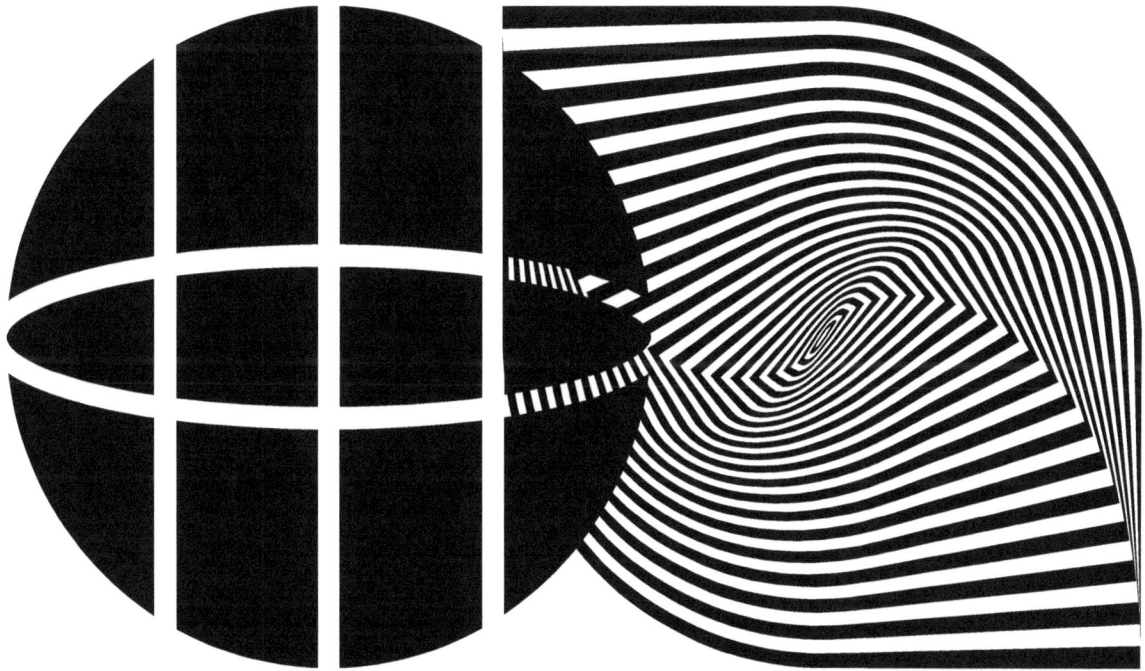

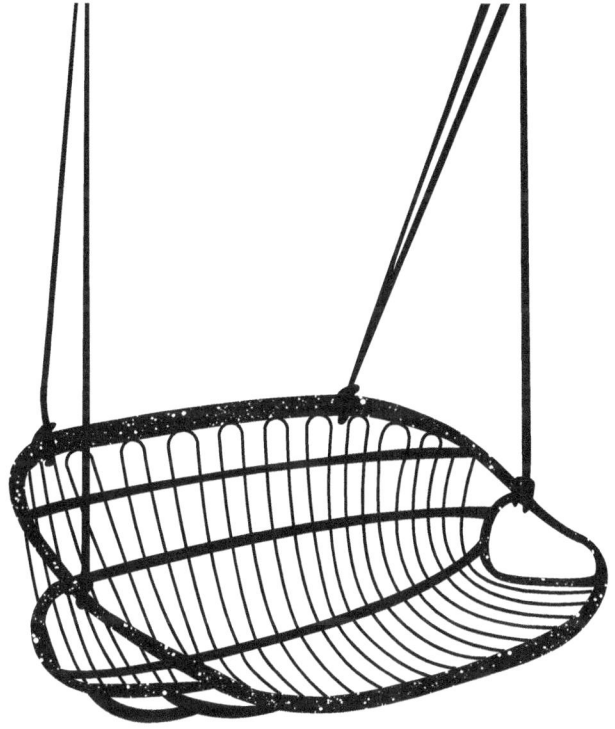

LOUNGE

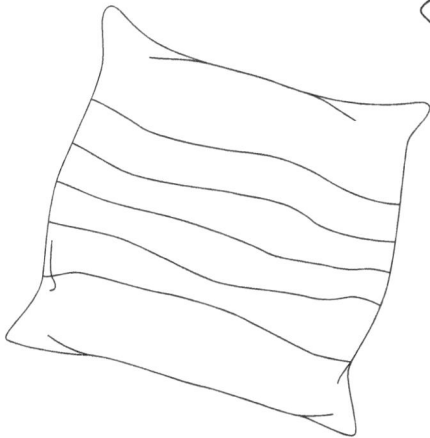

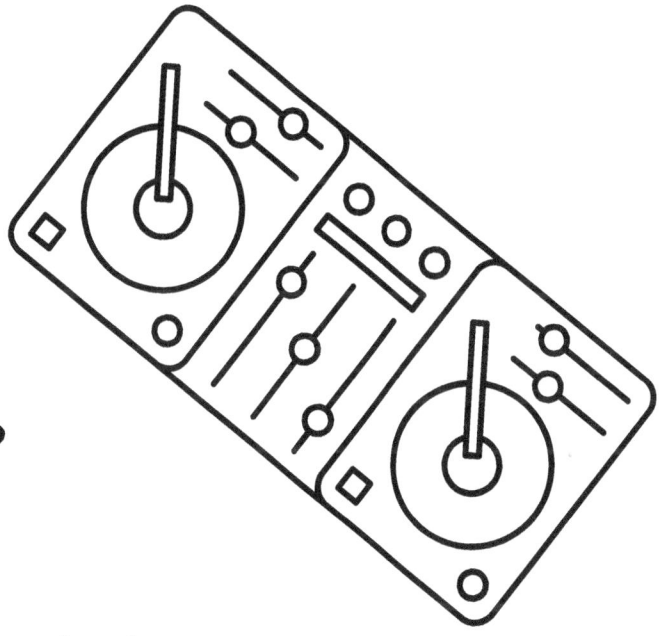

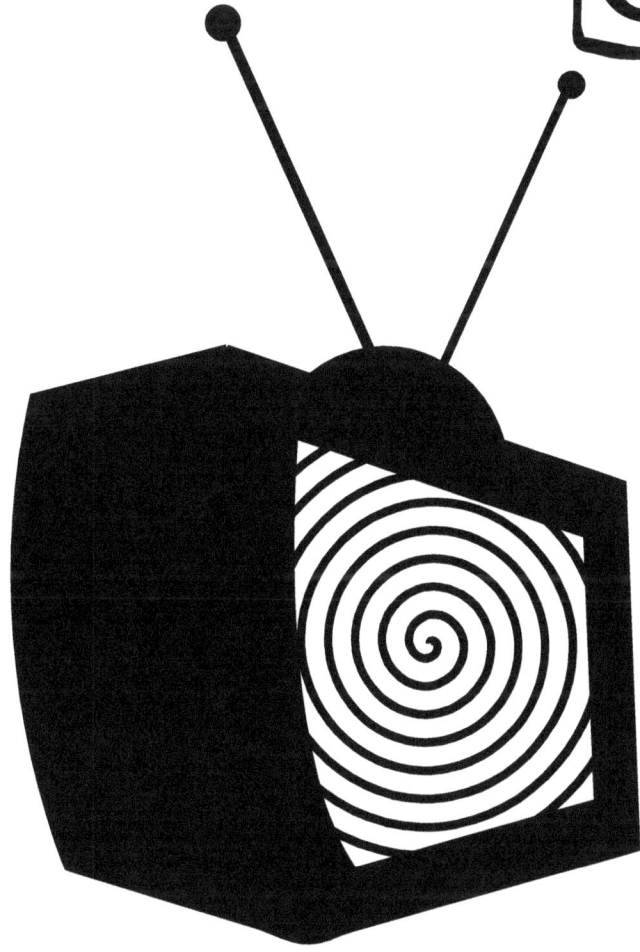

ULTIMATE RETRO DISCO DANCE PARTY

www.ingramcontent.com/pod-product-compliance
Lightning Source LLC
Chambersburg PA
CBHW081238020426
42331CB00029B/3050